Jeanne B. Becijos

A Festival of Folktales

Stories for Language Learning

Dominie Press, Inc.

Publisher: Raymond Yuen
Project Editor: Christa Malone
Text Illustrator: Rosalie Christensen
Text Designer: Becky Colgan
Cover Designer: Natalie Chupil

Published by:

🎕 **Dominie Press, Inc.**
1949 Kellogg Avenue
Carlsbad, California 92008 USA

www.dominie.com

ISBN 1-56270-048-0
Printed in the U.S.A.
2 3 4 5 6 W 06 05 04

Contents

Introduction _____

A *Festival of Folktales* is a collection of folktales from countries that represent different areas of the world. The stories are appropriate for ESL, bilingual, and general education students in elementary grades, junior high, high school, and adult basic education. The text provides interesting and motivating reading for advanced beginning/low intermediate ESL students. It is also appropriate for regular third-grade students. The material is presented using whole language, including a variety of listening, speaking, reading, and writing activities relating to the folktales. In accordance with the theories in Natural Approach, vocabulary and grammatical structures are introduced in written and pictorial context. The stories are presented in three segments: Into, Through, and Beyond. This format invites the students to become involved in the literature. The folktales were selected to portray positive male and female role models and to represent groups from various cultures around the world.

The lessons can be used in any sequence. They are not presented in order of difficulty, and they do not rely on the students having completed one unit in order to study the next.

To facilitate instruction of the material, use the following information and teaching suggestions to correlate with each section of a tale.

INTO

Knowing the Area

To familiarize the student with the geographic location of each folktale's country of origin, this section includes questions that relate to the continent of the country and the country's relationship to nearby lands. Maps are used in the text. A classroom map or globe would be helpful for introducing the textbook and each lesson. You may wish to review the continents and major countries with the class before you start the book. If possible, guide the students in marking each country as it is encountered in the reading. You may want to make comparisons regarding size and location between new countries and countries previously studied.

Getting Ready for the Folktale

After the students are familiar with the country of the folktale, the next section prepares the student for the story itself. This section includes vocabulary, concepts, and themes that will be presented in the story. A unique exercise in this section is the Problem Solving activity. Students are introduced to a problem that is similar to the major conflict in the folktale. Utilizing critical thinking skills, students brainstorm several possible solutions to the problem, then decide on the best course of action. Students may wish to complete this activity with a partner or in a small group. Also included in this section is a journal topic. The students write their personal reactions to a theme or aspect of the upcoming folktale. Completing these exercises helps the students focus on the upcoming material. In addition, it provides an opportunity to relate previous knowledge to new information.

THROUGH

The stories can be presented to the students in many different ways. You may wish to use one or a combination of the following methods to introduce the story:

- You or a student reads aloud the folktale as the class follows along in the book. You may wish to ask questions intermittently in order to check comprehension.

- Students read the story with a partner, taking turns reading aloud.

- Ask a question about the story, or have a student make a prediction about the story. Then assign the students three or more paragraphs to read silently with the question or prediction in mind. After reading is finished, answer the question or verify the prediction.

Story Summary/Language Exercises

A story summary is provided for the student to complete in order to solidify plot and characters in the student's mind. The summary is combined with a language exercise that focuses on a particular grammar, spelling, or writing skills. The concept is explained with examples. Students may work with a small group, with a partner, or individually on this assignment.

Deeper Understanding

These questions require higher-level thinking skills. You may wish to answer these as a class, individually as a written assignment, or with partners or small groups. Remind the students that these questions often require extra thought; the answers will not be found word-for-word in the story.

Theme

Each story has a sentence to complete that relates to the theme of the story. In this way, students are guided into the answer. Students may work as a class, with a small group or partner, or independently.

BEYOND

The activities in this segment solidify the folktale in the students' minds and build additional skills. The vocabulary games help reinforce vocabulary from the stories. The creative projects give the students an opportunity to synthesize their learning and practice creativity. When possible, exhibit the projects in the room to help build the students' self-esteem. Each folktale also includes a Role-Play activity in which the students complete a scene from the story with a partner. You may wish to have all students role-play with their partners at one time, or have partners present their role-plays in front of the class.

The Mountain Lion and the Cricket _____

INTO

Knowing the Area

"The Mountain Lion and the Cricket" is a folktale from Bolivia.

1. On which continent is Bolivia?
2. Name three countries next to Bolivia.

Vocabulary

The folktale "The Mountain Lion and the Cricket" tells of a battle between mammals and insects. Below are the names of different mammals and insects. Write each name in the correct category.

bear ant bee sheep

llama mountain lion cricket jaguar

mosquito rabbit

Mammals		Insects	
_____	_____	_____	_____
_____	_____	_____	_____
_____	_____	_____	_____
_____	_____	_____	_____

Problem Solving

In the story, one of the animals brags. He says he is better than all the other animals. Imagine that you know someone who brags a lot. He always says that he is better than you. List three or more ways to solve this problem.

Journal

Which animal is the king of the mammals? Which animal is the king of the insects? Explain your answers.

THROUGH

The Indians in Bolivia tell this tale about a fight between a mountain lion and a cricket.

The Mountain Lion and the Cricket

The mountain lion is the king of the mammals. He is strong. He is also very proud of himself. People and animals are afraid of him.

One day a cricket was drinking at a river. A mountain lion came to the river to drink, too.

"Move away," said the mountain lion. "I want to drink alone."

"I don't have to move. You are the king of the mammals. But I am the king of the insects. I have a right to drink."

The mountain lion laughed. "You weak little animal! I can kill you with one hit of my paw." The lion raised his paw. He was going to hit the cricket.

"Wait! I have an idea," said the cricket. "I dare you to fight. Tomorrow, bring an army of mammals to the river. I will bring an army of insects."

"You fool! Do you want your friends to die? Well, we will come tomorrow. I will bring all of my friends: the strongest animals, the fastest animals, the biggest animals, and many more." The mountain lion laughed again. He hit the ground with his tail. The cricket quickly jumped out of the way.

The next day, all of the mammals came to the river. There were many strong, fast, and big animals: bulls, bears, rabbits, sheep, llamas, jaguars, and others. "Thank you for coming, my friends," said the mountain lion. "Where is the cricket's army?"

The cricket jumped out of a bush.

THE MOUNTAIN LION AND THE CRICKET

"Where are your friends?" asked the mountain lion. "Are they afraid? You should be afraid, too."

"They are here," said the cricket. "Are you ready?"

"We are ready." The mountain lion smiled.

"Then the attack begins!" cried the cricket.

Suddenly, millions of insects appeared. They came out of the trees and the bushes. There were ants, bees, crickets, mosquitoes, and many others. Clouds of insects hid the sun. The little animals attacked the big animals. They attacked the mammals' eyes, ears, and mouths.

The mammals tried to fight the insects. But they couldn't see them or hear them. The mammals' ears and eyes hurt too much.

The battle lasted only a few minutes. "Stop! Stop the attack!" said the mountain lion. He had thousands of insects all over his body.

The mammals ran to the river. They jumped into the water to escape the attack. The cricket's army of insects had won.

The Indians say, "When little ones unite, they can win against someone who is stronger and bigger."

Story Summary and Language

Indefinite articles: Use the indefinite article *a* before nouns that start with a consonant sound. Use the indefinite article *an* before nouns that start with a vowel sound. Here are some examples:

an apple	a house	an honest man	a uniform

Complete the story summary. Use *a* or *an* in each blank.

One day, the mountain lion and the cricket had _____ fight. The
                                                    A
mountain lion said the cricket was weak. The cricket had _____ idea.
                                                          B
He dared the mountain lion. The cricket said, "I will bring _____
                                                             C
army of insects to the river. You bring _____ army of mammals."
                                         D

The next day, all the mammals came to the river. The strongest and biggest mammals were there. Then the cricket came out of _____ bush. He called to his army of ants, bees, and other insects. There was _____ attack by the insects. The insects bit the mammals' ears, eyes, and mouths. The mammals ran to the water. The little insects had won the battle.

Deeper Understanding

Answer the questions.

1. Why did the lion think he was better than the cricket?
2. Why did the cricket's army win?
3. What do you think the mountain lion will do the next time he sees the cricket?
4. Sometimes, a group of weaker ones wins against a stronger one. Give an example from history.
5. Find your favorite lines in the story. Read them to a partner or write them down. What do you like about these lines?
6. How did you solve the problem of the person who brags? How did the cricket solve the problem of the mountain lion who bragged? Compare the two solutions.

Theme

Complete this sentence. It is about the main idea of the story.

When smaller, weaker ones work together, _____.

Game

Play baseball: Everyone in the class writes ten questions about the story. One person, a moderator, collects the questions and draws a baseball diamond on the board. The class divides into two teams. The moderator asks a team a question. For each correct answer, the team moves forward to a base. The team scores a point when a runner gets to home base. Three wrong answers, and the other team has the chance to answer questions and score points.

Project

Make a *diorama*, or scene, of the folktale. Use a small box. Create a scene from the story inside the box. Use rocks, dirt, clay, magazine pictures, and other materials.

Role-Play

This is a scene from the beginning of the story. The mountain lion and the cricket are arguing. Role-play with a partner. Finish the scene with two or more lines.

Mountain Lion: Move away! I want to drink alone.

Cricket: I have a right to drink.

Mountain Lion:

Cricket:

The Poor Man and His Three Sons

Knowing the Area

"The Poor Man and His Three Sons" is a tale from the Philippines.

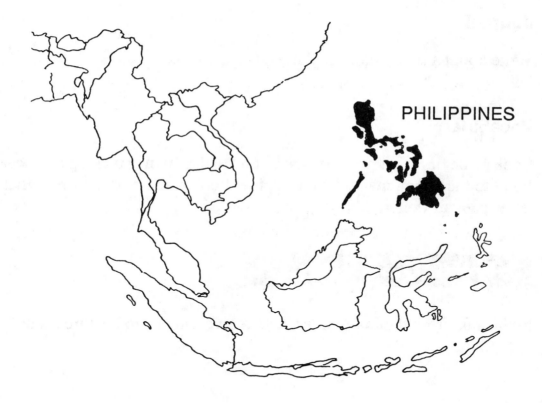

PHILIPPINES

1. Find the Philippines. Which continent is close to the Philippines?
2. Which ocean are the Philippine islands in?

Discussion

Animals are important to the farmers in the Philippines. How do these animals help farmers?

| horse | rooster | ox | cat |

Problem Solving

In the story "The Poor Man and His Three Sons," the three sons must earn money. How can you earn money? List three or more ways.

Journal

Write about a time you earned money.

Vocabulary

Look at the first picture in the story. Point to the **farmer** picking the **rice**. Point to the young man with the **scythe**. Look at the next picture. What is the **rooster** doing?

THROUGH

In this tale from the Philippines, a man gives advice to his three sons.

The Poor Man and His Three Sons

Long ago in the Philippines, a poor farmer lived with his three sons. The man had worked hard all his life. But he had no gold. His riches were his three sons.

One day, the farmer was very sick. He knew that he was dying. He called his sons to his bed. "My sons, I will die soon. I have no gold. But I do have something for you."

The sons listened sadly. They didn't want their father to die.

First, the father gave the oldest son a cat. Then he gave the second son a rooster. And to the youngest son he gave a scythe. The father said, "Travel far and wide. Find the right place to trade the rooster, the cat, and the scythe. Then you will be happy."

The sons thanked their father for the gifts. The father spoke no more. He had died.

Months passed. Life was hard for the sons. The farm was on poor land. There were no horses or oxen on the farm. The sons had little food to eat.

"Father said to trade the cat," said the oldest son. "But who wants to trade for a cat? Everyone on the island has a cat."

"Father said to travel far and wide," said the youngest son. "I will start tomorrow." The youngest son left his brothers. He took the scythe with him. He traveled for days and days. At last he came to a small island. There he saw some farmers picking rice. He was surprised. They were picking the rice with their hands.

"May I help you? I can cut the rice fast." The youngest son started cutting the rice with his scythe.

The men were surprised. They had never seen a scythe before. You can cut rice so quickly!" the men said. "What is that in your hand?"

The youngest son said, "It is a scythe. My father gave it to me."

The men talked quietly together. Then they said, "We want to trade for your scythe. We will give you gold."

The youngest son thought for a moment. Then he said, "I will trade with you." He gave the scythe to the men. Then the young man traveled home. He showed his brothers the riches.

"I can't believe it!" said the middle son. "Father was right. You need to find the right place to trade."

The next day, the middle son traveled far and wide. He took his rooster with him. At last he found a village without roosters. He slept in

the street with his rooster. When the sun came up, the rooster crowed. People looked out their windows. "What is that?" they asked.

The middle son answered, "It is my rooster. He is crowing. He wakes me every morning." The people wanted the rooster for their village. They offered gold to the middle son. Happily, the young man took the gold. He returned home rich and happy.

The oldest son said to his brothers, "I don't think I can trade my cat. But my father wanted me to try." He traveled for days and months. At last he came to an island with no cats. The island had problems with rats. The son put his cat down. The cat ran after the rats. Soon there were no more rats.

The people said, "We must have this cat! Will you trade for him?"

"Yes, I will," said the son with a smile. The people gave the young man a bag of gold.

The oldest son went home. He showed his riches to his brothers. The three sons lived happily for many more years.

Story Summary and Language

Rewrite the paragraphs below. Add the missing periods. Begin each new sentence with a capital letter. Remember, each sentence needs a subject and a verb.

a man was dying he gave his three sons a rooster, a cat, and a scythe he told his sons to find the right place to trade the gifts then the father died

the youngest son left with his scythe he found some farmers picking rice with their hands the son began to cut rice with his scythe the farmers traded gold for the scythe the middle son then went to a town with no roosters he traded his rooster to the people finally the oldest son traveled with his cat he found a place with no cats and traded his cat the three sons were happy

Deeper Understanding

Answer the questions.

1. What advice did the father give his sons?
2. Why did the people want the oldest son's cat?
3. Do people still trade today? Explain.
4. Find one or more interesting lines in the story. Read them to a partner or write them down. What do you like about these lines?
5. How did you solve the problem of earning money? How did the sons earn money? Compare the two ways to make money. Which do you like better?

Theme

Complete this sentence. It tells about the story's main idea.

Listen to _____.

BEYOND

Game

Play a game with names of animals. Divide the class into pairs or small groups. See how many names of animals each group can list in fifteen minutes. Pass the paper around the group so that each person can answer. Use a dictionary for spelling. When you are finished, put an asterisk (*) next to the animals that help people.

Project

Imagine that you want to sell or trade a scythe, a cat, or a rooster. Create an ad. Draw a picture of the object or animal. Describe it. Write that you want to sell or trade it. Work alone, with a partner, or in a small group.

Role-Play

This is a scene from the story. The middle son wants to trade his rooster. Role-play with a partner. What happens next? Write two or more lines.

Villager: What is making all that noise?

Son: It's my rooster.

Villager: What is it doing?

Son: It's crowing.

Villager: Why is it crowing?

Son:

Villager:

Two Merchants _____

Knowing the Area

"Two Merchants" is a Persian folktale. Today, the land of Persia is called Iran.

1. Is Iran on the continent of Africa, Asia, Australia, Europe, North America, or South America?
2. What country is north of Iran?
3. What country is west of Iran?

List

Why do people lie? List five reasons.

Vocabulary

These words are from the story. Match each word with its action.

Words	Actions
___ 1. merchant	A. eats cheese
___ 2. mouse	B. sells things
___ 3. iron	C. flies in the sky
___ 4. eagle	D. used for making tools

Problem Solving

In the story "Two Merchants," a man's friend lies to him. Imagine you have a friend who tells you a lie. List three or more ways to solve this problem.

Journal

Is it all right to lie to a friend? Explain.

THROUGH

In this Persian story, a man lies to his friend.

Two Merchants

Long ago there was a poor merchant. He sold iron to people for tools. One day, he had to go on a trip. But he didn't want to leave the iron in his house. Maybe someone would steal it.

"I know!" said the merchant. "I will leave the iron at the house of my friend. He will watch it for me." The merchant took the 600 pounds of iron to his friend's house.

A week later, the friend needed money. "I really need some money. But I have nothing to sell." Then he thought about the merchant's iron. The iron was in a corner of his house. "I can sell the iron. But what do I tell my friend? Maybe I can lie to him about it. He will believe me. He is my friend." The friend sold the merchant's iron. He put the money in a safe place.

In three days, the merchant returned. He went to his friend's house. "Thank you for watching my iron. I will take it now."

The friend said, "Oh, I have terrible news for you! I put the iron in the corner. One night, the mice were hungry. They ate all the iron."

The merchant showed no surprise. "Is that right? I'm sorry to hear it. But I know mice love iron. Also, their teeth are very sharp. They can eat iron easily."

The friend was happy. He thought his friend believed him. As the merchant left, he saw his friend's little boy. The boy was playing a game outside. The merchant took the boy to the merchant's home. The little boy was crying. He wanted his family. The merchant gave candy to the boy. The child stopped crying.

A few minutes later, the friend came to the merchant's door. The friend was worried. "Did you see my son? He is gone. I can't find him."

The merchant said, "I think I did see him. I saw an eagle carrying a boy."

"But that is impossible!" cried his friend. "An eagle can't carry a boy!"

The merchant laughed. "It seems impossible. But strange things happen in this town. A mouse eats 600 pounds of iron. An eagle carries a little boy. It's hard to believe. But it must be true."

The friend looked down at the ground. He understood. The merchant was teaching him a lesson.

"You are right. It is impossible for a mouse to eat iron. I lied to you. I sold your iron. But I will give you all the money. Please, return my son. He is more important than the money."

The merchant agreed. The friend went home. He found the money. Then he gave it to the merchant. The merchant went to get the boy. He returned the son to his father. The father and son were happy to be together again.

Story Summary and Language

Contractions: A *contraction* is a short form of two words. Here are some common contractions. The two words for each contraction are in parentheses ().

can't (can not)   it's (it is)

didn't (did not)   that's (that is)

I'm (I am)   you're (you are)

Write the missing contractions in the story summary.

A merchant _____ want to leave his iron in his house. He asked

     A
a friend to watch it. While the merchant was gone, his friend sold the iron. The merchant returned. His friend said that mice ate the iron. The merchant said, " _____ sorry to hear it."

          B

The merchant took his friend's little boy. His friend came to the merchant's house. "Did you see my son? I _____ find him." The

                   C
merchant said, "I saw an eagle carry a boy." The friend said, "_____

                        D
impossible!" The merchant said, " _____ hard to believe. But this is

              E
a strange town." The friend understood. " _____ right. I lied to you."

                   F
The friend returned the money and the merchant returned the son.

Deeper Understanding

Answer the questions.

1. Why did the friend lie to the merchant?
2. Why did the merchant say, "I know mice love iron"?
3. Why did the merchant take his friend's little boy?
4. Do you think the merchant and his friend continued to be friends? Explain.
5. Find some interesting lines in the story. Read them to a partner or write them down. What do you like about these lines?
6. How did you solve the problem of your friend's lie? How did the merchant solve the problem of his friend's lie? Compare the two solutions.

Theme

Complete this sentence about the story's main idea.

Lying _____.

BEYOND

Game

Play the game of Win, Lose, or Draw with vocabulary from the story. Divide the class into two teams. One team writes a word on a piece of paper. Then a member of the second team goes to the chalkboard and draws a picture for that word. The second team looks at the picture and guesses the word. See how long it takes the team to guess the word. Then the first team draws and guesses a word. The team that guesses its word in the shorter amount of time scores a point.

Project

Hold a trial for the merchant's friend. The friend is on trial because he stole the merchant's iron. You need a judge, two lawyers, the friend, the merchant, and the little boy as witness. Write the script for the trial, or act out the trial without a script.

Role-Play

This is a scene from the end of the story. The friend is looking for his son. Role-play with a partner. Finish the scene with two or more lines.

Friend: Did you see my son? He is gone.

Merchant: I saw an eagle carrying a boy.

Friend: That's impossible!

Merchant: This is a strange town. Mice eat iron and an eagle carries a boy.

Friend:

Merchant:

Ma Liang and His Magic Brush _____

INTO

Knowing the Area

"Ma Liang and His Magic Brush" is a folktale from China.

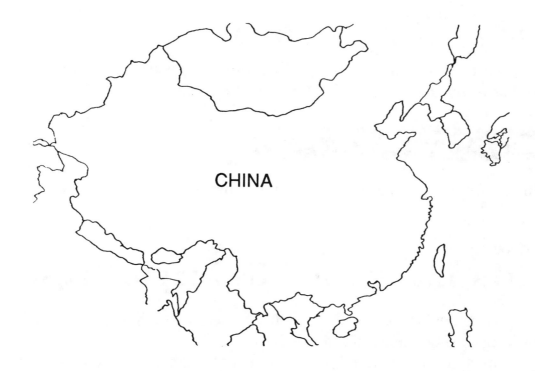

CHINA

1. Is China on the continent of Australia, North America, South America, Europe, Asia, or Africa?
2. Name three countries next to China.

Survey

The boy in this story has a magic paintbrush. He paints something, and it becomes real.

Do a survey of your class. Ask each person, "What would you draw with a magic brush?" Put the answers in categories.

Problem Solving

The boy in this story has no money to buy art materials. He wants to paint, but he can't buy a brush or paper or ink. How can he solve his problem? List three or more ways.

Journal

The boy in this folktale doesn't give up easily. He keeps trying, even when he has problems. Do you give up easily? Explain.

THROUGH

In this Chinese tale, a poor boy wants to draw.

Ma Liang and His Magic Brush

Ma Liang's parents died when he was young. The boy lived by picking up wood and pulling weeds.

One day, he was weeding the garden of a school. There he saw the master and his students. The master was showing his students how to paint. Instantly, Liang loved the beauty of the art. He truly wanted to paint. But he had no money to buy a paintbrush or paper.

Liang talked to the master of the school. "Please, can you lend me a brush? I want to paint."

The master was angry. "Go away! Painting is not for beggar boys."

Ma Liang left, but he did not give up. "A poor boy can draw. I will learn another way." He drew animals in the dirt with a stick. He used water to draw fish on the rocks. People saw his pictures. They thought his drawings were amazing. The birds in his pictures seemed ready to fly away. The fish appeared ready to swim in the water.

Ma Liang still hoped to paint with a brush. He thought about it every day. One night, Liang had a dream. In the dream, an old man came to Liang. The man gave Liang a brush.

"Be careful with this brush," said the Old One. "It is magic."

Ma Liang woke up and looked. The paintbrush was in his hand!

For three days, Liang bought no rice. He saved his money. At last he could buy ink and paper. The boy painted a bird with his magic brush. When he finished, the bird opened its eyes. Then it moved its wings and flew into the sky! Ma Liang painted a fish. The fish jumped in the water and swam away. People saw the boy's magic. They brought him paper. With his magic brush, Liang helped the poor people. He painted a hoe for a farmer. He painted an oil lamp for an old woman. He painted rice for a young mother.

The emperor in his palace learned of Ma Liang. He sent his guards to get the young artist. Ma Liang didn't want to go. He had heard bad stories about the emperor. The emperor was very cruel to poor people. But the guards forced Liang to go to the palace.

Ma Liang said to himself, "I will never serve this man."

The emperor told Ma Liang to paint a beautiful gold dragon. Instead, Ma Liang painted a green frog. The emperor told the boy to paint a lovely singing bird. Instead, Liang painted a brown chicken. The frog and the chicken made a lot of noise. They ran around and broke expensive objects. The guards couldn't catch the animals.

The emperor was very angry. He took away Ma Liang's magic brush. With the brush, the emperor drew a mountain of gold. But when he finished, he had only a pile of rocks. He tried again to make gold. This time, the gold became a yellow serpent. Afraid, the emperor dropped the brush. The large serpent attacked the emperor. The guards ran to save their leader. They killed the serpent with their swords. With all the noise, no one saw Ma Liang. The boy picked up his magic brush. Then he quickly ran out of the palace.

What happened to Ma Liang and his magic brush? No one is sure. Some say he went back to help his village. Others say he went all over China to paint for the poor.

Story Summary and Language

Homonyms: Homonyms are words that sound the same but have different meanings and spellings. For example, *be* and *bee* are homonyms, and *sea* and *see* are homonyms.

Finish the story summary. Use the correct homonym in each sentence.

1. Ma Liang lived ___ (buy, by) picking up wood and pulling weeds.
2. He wanted to paint, but he had no money to ___ (buy, by) a brush or paper.
3. Liang drew in the dirt. People said "___ (Your, You're) pictures are amazing."
4. In the boy's dream, an old man said, "___ (Your, You're) going to get a magic brush."
5. With his magic brush, Liang painted a bird. The bird opened ___ (its, it's) eyes and flew away.
6. The people saw the bird and said, "___ (Its, It's) a real bird!"
7. The cruel emperor wanted Ma Liang to paint for him. Ma Liang said to himself, "___ (Know, No), I will not serve this man."
8. Ma Liang escaped from the emperor. People don't ___ (know, no) what happened to the boy.

Deeper Understanding

Answer the questions.

1. Would you like to have the master from this story as a teacher? Why or why not?
2. Did Ma Liang give up easily when he had a problem? Explain.
3. Why didn't the brush work for the emperor?
4. Read the story's last paragraph again. Where do you think Ma Liang went? Explain your answer.
5. Write down one or more sentences from the story that show the personality of Ma Liang. Read the sentences to a partner or write them in your journal.
6. How did you solve the problem of no money for art materials? How did Ma Liang solve the problem? Compare the two solutions. Which solution do you like better?

Theme

Complete this sentence about the story's main idea.

Don't give up because _____.

BEYOND

Game

In a small group, find ten difficult words from the story. Make cards from cardboard. Write each vocabulary word on one card. Write the definition or draw a picture of the word on another card. Then play Concentration with the cards: turn the cards over. Try to match each word with its picture or definition.

Project

Imagine that "Ma Liang and His Magic Brush" is a movie. Make a poster advertisement for the movie. Include the title, draw a picture, and write comments about the story. (Look in the newspaper for an example of a movie advertisement.)

Role-Play

In the story, Ma Liang does not want to paint for the emperor. Role-play with a partner. Finish the scene with two or more lines.

Emperor: I want you to paint a gold dragon for me.

Ma Liang: No, I don't want to paint for you.

Emperor: Why not?

Ma Liang:

Emperor:

The Caterpillar and the Crow

INTO

Knowing the Area

"The Caterpillar and the Crow" is a tale from Cambodia. Today, Cambodia is known as Kampuchea.

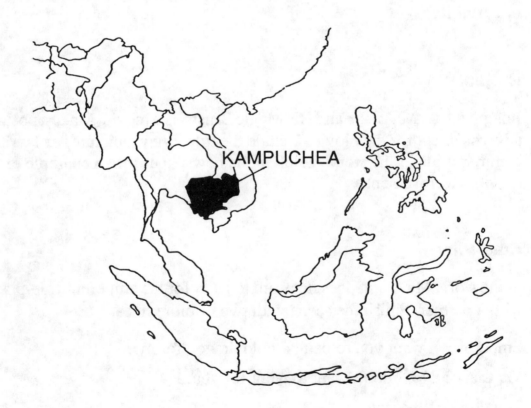

1. Is Kampuchea on the continent of Africa, Asia, Australia, Europe, North America, or South America?
2. Name three countries next to Kampuchea.

Chart

In the folktale "The Caterpillar and the Crow," a caterpillar talks about the sweetest, most bitter, worst-smelling, and best-smelling things in the world. Complete the chart below. List five ideas for each category.

Sweetest Things	Most Bitter Things
1.	1.
2.	2.
3.	3.
4.	4.
5.	5.
Best-Smelling Things	**Worst-Smelling Things**
1.	1.
2.	2.
3.	3.
4.	4.
5.	5.

Problem Solving

In the story "The Caterpillar and the Crow," the caterpillar must win against the crow. The crow is bigger and stronger, but he is not smarter.

Imagine that you must win against someone. That person is bigger and stronger than you. What can you do to win? List three or more ways to solve the problem.

Journal

Do you like riddles? Why or why not? Write a riddle in your journal. Tell the riddle to the class.

THROUGH

This folktale from the land of Cambodia tells of a battle between a crow and a caterpillar.

The Caterpillar and the Crow

It was a beautiful, sunny day. The sky was blue. There were no clouds. A caterpillar was looking for a good breakfast. He searched high and low. At last he found a delicious leaf. It was a big green leaf of his favorite tree.

As he started to eat, a black shadow fell on the leaf. The caterpillar looked up. A crow was flying above him. The big black bird landed next to the caterpillar. The caterpillar pretended not to see the bird. He calmly ate his breakfast.

"Enjoy your food, caterpillar. Then you will be a bigger breakfast for me," said the crow.

The caterpillar stopped eating. He looked up. "Good morning, crow. Do you like riddles?"

The crow said, "Of course. I am good at riddles."

"Then I will tell you one," said the caterpillar. "If you answer it, then you will enjoy your breakfast more. If you can't answer it, then you will look for breakfast in a new place."

"Very well," said the crow. "First my mind will be happy. Then my stomach will be happy."

"Name the sweetest thing in the world," said the caterpillar.

"That is too easy," answered the crow. "The sweetest thing is sugar."

"Next, name the most bitter thing in the world," said the caterpillar.

"The most bitter thing is a lemon. Don't you have a difficult question?" asked the crow.

"All right. What is the worst-smelling thing in the world?" asked the caterpillar.

"The worst-smelling thing is manure. This riddle is boring. I know all the answers."

"Last, what is the best-smelling thing in the world?" asked the caterpillar.

"The best-smelling thing is the flower of the Champa tree," said the crow. "I answered your bad riddle. Now I can begin my breakfast." The bird picked up the caterpillar.

"Wait a minute! Not so fast," cried the caterpillar. "Your first answer is wrong. Your second answer is wrong. And your third and fourth answers are wrong, too."

The crow said, "But, I am right!"

"No, you are not," said the caterpillar. "I am very surprised. You don't know the correct answers. The sweetest things in the world are loving, kind words. The most bitter things are cruel words. The worst-smelling thing is a bad name, a poor reputation. And a good name, a fine reputation, is the best-smelling thing in the world."

The crow was angry. He dropped the caterpillar. "All right. You win. I will look for breakfast in a new place." The crow flew away.

The caterpillar began to eat his leaf again. It was a beautiful day indeed.

Story Summary and Language

Spelling rule: Many words end this way: **consonant-vowel-consonant.** You may want to add a suffix to some of these words. Before adding the suffix, double the last consonant of the word. Here are two examples:

c v c
s t o p + e d = sto**pp**ed

c v c
s i t + i n g = si**tt**ing

Finish the sentences about the story. Write the correct form of each word and suffix in parentheses ().

1. One beautiful, _____ (sun + y) day, a caterpillar was looking for breakfast.
2. He saw a crow _____ (fly + ing) over him, but he pretended not to see the bird.
3. "Enjoy your food," said the crow. "Then you will be a _____ (big + er) breakfast for me."
4. The caterpillar _____ (stop + ed) eating and asked the crow a riddle.
5. The caterpillar _____ (want + ed) the crow to name the sweetest, most bitter, worst-smelling, and best-smelling things in the world.
6. The crow _____ (answer + ed): sugar, a lemon, manure, and the Champa tree flower.
7. The caterpillar _____ (explain + ed) the correct answers: loving words, cruel words, a bad name, and a good name.
8. The crow angrily _____ (drop + ed) the caterpillar and flew away.

Deeper Understanding

Answer the questions.

1. Did the caterpillar really feel calm? Or was he afraid? Explain.
2. Who is smarter, the caterpillar or the crow? Explain.
3. Is the riddle in the story a good riddle? Why or why not?
4. Do you agree with the caterpillar's answers to the riddle? Why or why not?
5. Find your favorite lines in the story. Read them to a partner or write them in your journal. What do you like about these lines?
6. How did you solve the problem of a stronger enemy? How did the caterpillar solve the problem of a stronger enemy? Compare the two solutions.

Theme

Complete this sentence about the story's main idea.

It is important to _____.

Game

Play a memory/speaking game with the class. The first person says the name of an animal. The next person repeats the name and then adds the name of a different animal. The third person repeats the two names and adds another one. Continue in the same way. The person who remembers all the names wins the game.

Project

Create puppets of the caterpillar and the crow. Use sticks, paper, paper plates, paper bags, socks, or other materials. Then act out the story with the two puppets.

Role-Play

This is a scene from the end of the story. The crow is trying to answer the riddle. Role-play with a partner. Finish the scene with four or more lines.

Caterpillar: What is the sweetest thing in the world?

Crow: That's easy. The sweetest thing is sugar.

Caterpillar: What is the most bitter thing in the world?

Crow: I know that. The most bitter thing is a lemon.

Caterpillar:

Crow:

Caterpillar:

Crow:

Csucskari

INTO

Knowing the Area

"Csucskari" is a folktale from Hungary.

1. Is Hungary on the continent of Africa, Australia, Asia, Europe, North America, or South America?
2. Name three countries next to Hungary.

Journal

In the folktale "Csucskari," there are soldiers, gypsies, a king, a princess, and a smith. Which of these would you like to be? Why?

Problem Solving

In this folktale, the father is old and has little money. His three sons want to help him. How can they help him? List three or more ways.

THROUGH

This folktale is about a brave young man. He wants to help the king and marry the princess.

Csucskari

Beyond the seven seas, a poor gypsy lived with his three sons. The old father had little money. The sons told their father, "We know you have many troubles. We will leave to find our fortune." The father sadly told his sons good-bye.

As they were walking, the three young gypsies saw the king's soldiers. One soldier told the sons, "Listen, my friends. The king has a message for everyone, rich and poor, young and old. For many years there has been only darkness. The sun and moon have left the sky. The man who can fix the sun and moon in the sky will get half the kingdom. He will also marry the princess."

The three sons liked the idea. They went to the king's palace. The youngest son, Csucskari, made a contract with the king. The young man signed the contract in gold letters with his finger.

The three sons traveled. On their way, they talked to a wise old man. The man told them to go to the wild forest. There they would find a special

box. This box held the secret to fix the sun and moon. But first they had to pass through a dangerous land. This land was the home of dragons.

The three sons entered the land of the dragons. Soon they heard a terrible noise. In front of them there was a dragon with eight heads. Csucskari said, "Let me pass! I have come to fix the sun and the moon."

"No one passes by here! Prepare to fight," said the dragon. Csucskari fought the dragon with his sword. At last he won. The three young men continued their trip. Soon they heard more terrible noises. This time there was a dragon with ten heads. Again Csucskari fought the dragon and won.

The young men were almost to the wild forest. Then, in front of them, there was a dragon with twelve heads! The dragon said to Csucskari, "You won the fight against my two brothers. But you will not win against me."

The fight began. The dragon and Csucskari were equal in strength. The fight lasted two days. At the end of the second day, the youngest son said to the dragon, "I must win! I have to bring light to the kingdom." With a final blow, Csucskari won the fight.

Tired but happy, the three sons came to the wild forest. They found a box with twelve bees inside. The bees had the power to bring back the light. The young men then began their return trip to the palace. On the way, they stopped by the home of a smith. The oldest brother told the smith their adventures. The smith said, "I'm going to take the box from you. Then I can go to the palace for the reward." The three sons tried to stop the man. They could not. The smith was stronger than twenty men.

Csucskari saw that the smith wore a special shirt. When the man went to sleep, he took off his shirt. That night, Csucskari stole the special shirt. The smith was very angry when he woke up. He needed his shirt to be strong. The three sons took back their box of bees. The smith could not stop them.

The three young men went on their way. At last they came to the palace. Csucskari said to the king, "Good day to you, sir. I will now bring light to the land. And then I will marry the princess." The young man opened the box of bees. The twelve bees flew into the sky. Once again, the sun shone during the day, and the moon shone at night.

People from seven countries came to the royal wedding. Csucskari married the king's blond daughter. And the wedding feast went on for seven years and seven minutes.

Story Summary and Language

Present tense: Here is the conjugation for regular verbs in the *present tense:*

I work	we work
you work	you work
he/she/it works	they work

(Notice the *s* after the verb for *he/she/it*.)

Write the correct form of the verb in these sentences about the story.

1. The three sons _____ (leave, leaves) their father to find their fortune.
2. Soldiers _____ (tell, tells) the sons about the king's message: the man who can fix the sun and moon in the sky will get half the kingdom and marry the princess.
3. Csucskari _____ (sign, signs) a contract with the king.
4. A wise old man _____ (tell, tells) the young men to find a special box.
5. Csucskari _____ (win, wins) against dragons with eight heads and ten heads.
6. A twelve-headed dragon _____ (fight, fights) Csucskari for two days, but Csucskari wins.
7. The three sons _____ (find, finds) the special box of bees in the wild forest.
8. A smith _____ (steal, steals) the box, but Csucskari gets the box back.
9. Csucskari _____ (open, opens) the box of bees, and the sun and moon return to the sky.
10. Csucskari and the princess _____ (marry, marries), and the wedding lasts for seven years and seven minutes.

Deeper Understanding

Answer the questions.

1. What problem did the king have?
2. Which of the sons' adventures was the most dangerous? Explain.
3. How do you think the bees helped bring back the light?
4. Do you believe that the wedding really lasted seven years and seven minutes? Explain.
5. Write down one or more interesting sentences from the story. Read them to a partner or write them in your journal. Why did you choose these sentences?
6. How did you solve the problem of the poor father? How did the sons solve the problem? Compare the two solutions.

Theme

Complete this sentence about the main idea of the story.

To get what you want, you need to _____.

BEYOND

Game

In a small group, make a traveling game about the story. Include places such as the sons' home, the land of the dragons, the wild forest, the smith's house, and the palace. Each person writes down five questions about the story. One person collects the questions and asks them. For each correct answer, a person moves forward in the game. The first person to finish the trip to the palace wins.

Project

Design a wedding invitation to the marriage of Csucskari and the princess. Include the answers to who, what, when, and where in the invitation.

Role-Play

In the story, a wise old man tells the three sons about the wild forest, the special box, and the dangerous land. Role-play with a partner. Finish the scene.

Csucskari: How can we fix the sun and the moon in the sky?

Wise Old Man: Go to the wild forest. You will find a special box there.

Csucskari: What is inside the box?

Wise Old man:

Csucskari:

The Flying Head _____

Knowing the Area

"The Flying Head" is a Native American tale from the Iroquois tribe. The land of the Iroquois tribe is now part of the United States.

1. Is the United States on the continent of Africa, Asia, Australia, Europe, North America, or South America?
2. What country is north of the United States? What country is south of the United States?
3. Point to the northeastern part of the United States. The Iroquois people lived in this area. Which ocean is near?

Chart

The folktale "The Flying Head" is a story from the Iroquois tribe. The words below name things from the Iroquois way of life. Place each word in the correct category. Draw a picture next to each word.

eagle   bows and arrows   longhouse   rabbit   corn

stone   stick   deer   plants   fire

Living	Not Living

Problem Solving

In the folktale "The Flying Head," a monster eats all the plants and animals. Pretend you have this problem. List three or more ways to solve the problem.

Journal

The woman in this story is very brave. Name a brave person. What brave thing did he or she do?

THROUGH

Long ago, the Iroquois people lived by hunting and farming. Their homes were called longhouses. The longhouses were big and made from trees. Many Iroquois families lived in one longhouse.

In this folktale, a brave Iroquois woman helps her tribe.

The Flying Head

One stormy night, the Flying Head monster came to the land. It was a horrible monster. It had wings, but it had no body and no legs. It had a green tongue, black teeth, and two holes for its nose. Fire and smoke came out of the holes. Its skin was purple and gray. The monster could fly as high and fast as an eagle.

The Flying Head was very hungry. The first night, it ate all the corn in the fields. The next night, it came again. It ate all the rabbits in the land. Again the monster came. This time, it ate all the deer in the forest. The men tried to kill the monster. They used their bows and arrows. But nothing stopped the Flying Head. The monster tried to eat the men, so the men ran away.

All of the people were afraid. There were no more plants or animals. There were only people. What if the monster came for them?

That night, all the families left their homes. They ran to hide in the biggest longhouse. Everyone went except for one woman. She stayed alone in a longhouse with her baby. She had a plan to stop the monster. First, she fed the baby. Then she hid the little one in the house. Next, the woman made a big fire. She heated many large stones. The stones turned red with the heat.

The monster saw the smoke from the woman's longhouse. It flew down to her door to look. But the woman ignored the monster. She continued with her cooking. Using a big stick, she picked up a hot stone. She pretended to eat it.

"This is delicious!" she said. "I'm sorry that the others are not here. What a wonderful dinner!" She picked up another stone, then another. She passed the stones by her mouth. Then she put them on the floor. The monster didn't see her trick.

The monster wanted the wonderful food. He flew in and pushed away the woman. In one bite, the monster ate all the rocks in the fire. Suddenly, the monster screamed. All the nearby tribes heard the loud yells. The monster flew out of the longhouse. It yelled until the earth shook. Still screaming loudly, the monster finally flew away.

The young woman picked up her baby. She went to the door and looked out. At last the night was quiet. All of the people came to hear her story. They were amazed and happy at her trick.

The Flying Head never returned to the land of the Iroquois.

Story Summary and Language

Past progressive: Verbs in the *past progressive tense* show a continuing past action. Here is the form of the past progressive:

was/were + (verb) + *ing*

Here are examples of the past progressive:

The woman was cooking the rocks.
The monster was flying away.

Complete the story summary. Use the past progressive verbs from the box.

was screaming	were running	were living
was pretending	were coming	

Long ago, the Iroquois people _____ in longhouses. One night,
the Flying Head monster came to the land. It was horrible, with
wings, a green tongue, and black teeth. Smoke and fire _____ out of
its nose holes.

The Flying Head was very hungry. It ate the corn, the rabbits, and
the deer. The people were afraid. That night, all the families _____
to hide in one longhouse. Only one woman stayed. She had a plan.
She heated stones in a fire. Then the monster came. It watched the
woman. She _____ to eat the stones. The monster flew in and ate all
the stones in the fire. For a long time after, the monster _____. Then
it flew away. The people were happy about the woman's trick.

Deeper Understanding

Answer the questions.

1. Why were the people afraid of the monster?
2. Do you think the woman in the story was brave? Explain.
3. Why did the woman feed the baby before she hid it?
4. In the end, why was the monster yelling so loudly?
5. Find your favorite lines in the story. Read them to a partner or write them down. What do you like about these lines?
6. How did you solve the problem of the monster? How did the woman in the story solve the problem? Compare the two solutions.

Theme

Complete this sentence about the story's main idea.

Often, you can solve a problem by _____.

BEYOND

Game

Play Password with vocabulary from the story. Each member of the class writes down five words from the story. One person, a moderator, collects the words. The class divides into two or more groups. The moderator chooses a word and shows it to a player from each group. The players give their teams one-word clues. The teams try to guess the word.

Project

Create your own monster. Write about it. Describe these things about the monster:

- its colors
- its face
- its body
- what it eats
- what it can do
- where it lives
- its name

Make your monster. Use an old cereal box, paper, glue, and objects around the house.

Role-Play

This is a scene from the end of the story. The people are happy that the woman tricked the monster. Role-play with a partner. Finish the scene with two or more lines.

Neighbor: How wonderful! You scared away the monster.

Woman: I wanted to protect my child from the Flying Head.

Neighbor: How did you scare the monster away?

Woman:

Neighbor:

The Girl Who Changed into a Kangaroo

INTO

Knowing the Area

"The Girl Who Changed into a Kangaroo" is a folktale from Australia.

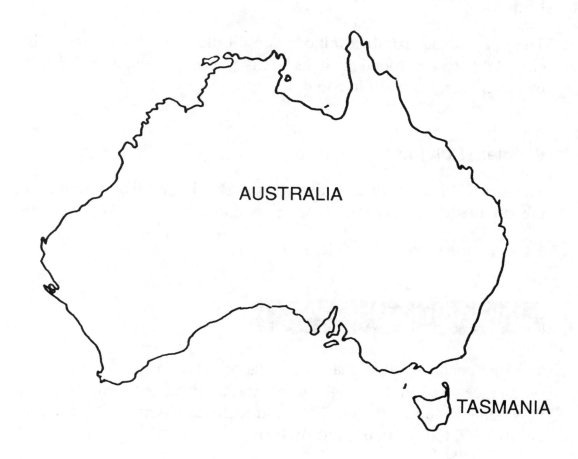

1. Which continent is north of the continent of Australia?
2. Which oceans are around Australia?

Cluster

Kangaroos live in Australia. What does *kangaroo* make you think of? Write the words by the lines.

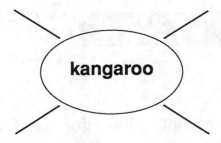

List

The girl in this Australian folktale doesn't like to do her chores. What chores do you do around the house? List the chores. Put an asterisk (*) by the chores you don't like to do.

Problem Solving

The girl in this story doesn't like chores. She doesn't like to find food, prepare the food, and take care of the children.

How can she solve this problem? List three or more ways.

THROUGH

The first people of Australia were the aborigines. Possibly they are the oldest race on earth. Long ago, the aborigines lived on the plains. There they hunted and found food. They told each other stories. These stories are still told today. Here is one of them.

The Girl Who Changed into a Kangaroo

Long, long ago, there was an unhappy girl. She didn't like women's work. Every day, the women worked very hard. And every day, the work was always the same. The girl didn't like to dig up plants for food. She didn't like to look for insects to eat. She didn't like to prepare the meals. And she didn't like to take care of the young children. She wanted to do the work of the men and boys. Their lives seemed more free. Every day, the men and boys left the camp to hunt for food. To the girl, the men's work was more exciting.

One day, the girl decided to escape her boring life. She left her camp while her father was away hunting. She ran and ran. She came to a valley with a stream. The girl didn't light a fire. She was afraid her father would see the fire. Then he would look for her. That night, she slept near the stream. She stayed in the valley for many days. There were plants and insects to eat. Every day, the girl climbed a hill and looked for her father. One day, she saw him in the distance. The girl smiled to herself. She knew her father couldn't find her. She had hidden her tracks well.

More days passed. The girl didn't see her father again. At last, the girl felt safe. She made a fire with sticks. Then she cooked some plants and insects. That night, she slept in peace. But the girl's father had not gone away. He had camped near the hills. In the night, he saw the light of the girl's fire. The next day, he walked to the valley. He hid behind a rock. He watched his daughter look for insects in the trees. Then he went to get her. The girl saw him and screamed. She ran to a group of trees. She hid behind a white tree. The tree was broken and had no top. At first, the father did not see his daughter. Then he saw her hiding.

The girl was afraid. She didn't want to return to her old way of life. Suddenly, she remembered some magic words. Her grandmother had told her this magic long ago. She held onto the tree. Then she quickly said the magic words. There was a loud noise. The tree came out of the ground. The girl held on as the tree jumped and leaped down the valley. The father ran after the girl and the white tree. He ran and ran until he had to stop. His body could not run anymore. Angrily, he watched the tree hop out of view.

Soon the girl was far, far away from her father. She was safe. But how could she stop the tree? She didn't know the magic words. She kept

THE GIRL WHO CHANGED INTO A KANGAROO

jumping until the tree became part of her. Her legs grew long and strong. Her arms became short.

It is said that this girl was the first kangaroo. The kangaroo is both dark and white. It has the colors of the dark girl and the white tree. The kangaroo also likes to jump and be free.

Story Summary and Language

Write the words in the correct order. Make sentences. The sentences are a summary of the story.

1. didn't like / an aborigine girl / her work / long ago / .
2. wanted / men's work / the girl / to do / .
3. the girl / to / a valley / ran away / .
4. tried / her father / his daughter / to find / .
5. found / because of her fire / his daughter / the father / .
6. behind / hid / a tree / the girl / .
7. magic words / the girl / began to jump / and the tree / said / .
8. changed / a kangaroo / into / the girl / .

Deeper Understanding

Answer the questions.

1. Why didn't the girl in the story like her work?
2. Today, do we have separate "men's work" and "women's work"? Explain.
3. Did you feel sorry for the father at the end of this story? Explain.
4. Is the end of this story happy or sad? Explain.
5. Write down one or more sentences from the story that show action. Read them to a partner or write them in your journal. Why did you choose these sentences?
6. How did you solve the problem of the girl's chores? How did she solve the problem? Compare the two solutions. Which solution do you like better?

Theme

Complete this sentence about the story's main idea.

A person is unhappy if _____.

Game

Play bingo with words from the story. Fold a piece of paper into sixteen equal parts. (Fold the paper in half four times.) Write one word in each square of the paper. Write these words (but *not* in this same order): aborigine, plains, insect, hunt, boring, stream, valley, hill, hidden, tracks, stick, scream, daughter, leap, view, kangaroo. Choose a bingo caller. That person calls out the definitions of the words. Cover or mark each word when the caller says its definition. A person wins with four marked words in a row.

Project

Imagine that you could be an animal for one day. Which animal would you be? Write a story about this idea. Use this form:

An Animal for a Day

If I could be an animal for one day, I'd like to be a _____. I'd like to be this animal because _____. For fun I would _____.

Role-Play

In the story, the father found his daughter. Imagine that they talked to each other. Role-play with a partner. Finish the scene.

Father: Come back with me.

Girl: No, I don't want to.

Father: Why did you run away?

Girl:

Father:

Anya's Garden

INTO

Knowing the Area

"Anya's Garden" is a tale from India.

1. Is India on the continent of Africa, Asia, Australia, Europe, North America, or South America?
2. Name two countries next to India.

Problem Solving

In "Anya's Garden," Anya follows her husband to a new land. She leaves her country and home. Imagine that you must move to be with a loved one. You don't like the new place. List three ways to solve this problem.

Venn Diagram

Anya from the story first lives in a tropical garden. She then moves to a desert. Use the words in the box and copy the marked circles. Write the words that go with a tropical garden in one of the circles. Write the words that go with a desert in the other circle. In the middle section, write the words that can go with both a garden and a desert.

tall trees	sand	camels	rainfall	large flowers
palace	fountains	humid	towers	dry	pavilion

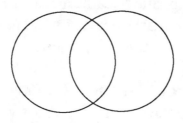

THROUGH

In this story from India, a young woman wants only to live in her beautiful garden.

Anya's Garden

Long ago in the land of India, there was a little girl named Anya. She lived in the middle of a beautiful garden. Anya had no parents. Servants looked after her. Every day, the girl walked through the tall green trees of her garden. She picked flowers of every color and threw them in the fountains. In the humid afternoons, Anya rested in her pavilion. She listened to the rainfall. Anya was always at peace in her lovely garden.

One day, an old man, a guru, came to her garden. He had a wise face. "Anya, my child. I was with your mother the day she died. You were only a baby. I promised her that I would give you one wish. You can have great wealth or great beauty. You can even be a princess. What wish do you choose?"

Anya thought about being wealthy, or beautiful, or powerful. None of these things promised happiness. She knew happiness already in her garden. "All my life I want to live in the middle of this beautiful garden."

The guru was surprised. "Is that all? Maybe someday you will want more than a garden. But you have made your wish. You will live always in the center of your garden. I promise." Then the guru went away.

The young girl grew up. She became a beautiful young woman. Men from near and far wanted to marry her. They fell in love with the peaceful happy girl. But Anya told all of the young men to go away. She didn't want to leave her garden.

One morning, Anya saw a stranger walking on a road outside her garden. He stopped and spoke to her. His words were kind and his smile was honest. Anya fell in love with the tall, handsome man.

The young man was Prince Kester from a faraway land. He visited Anya every day for a month. Then he asked, "Will you marry me? I love you, Anya. I want you to come with me to my home."

Anya looked down with tears in her eyes. What a difficult choice! She loved the prince, but she also loved her garden. At last she said, "I will come with you. But I may not be able to leave. A guru once gave me one wish. I said that I wanted to stay here in my garden forever."

The prince led Anya through a small gate in the garden wall. Nothing happened. The guru hadn't kept his promise. She was able to leave her garden.

Anya married the prince that same day. She loved Kester, but she still was sad to leave her garden. The husband and wife rode on camels to his kingdom in the desert. After weeks of traveling, they came to Kester's home. The palace was elegant with high marble towers. But there were no green trees or colorful flowers. Around the palace there was only the gold sand and hot, dry air of the desert.

That night Anya thought of her garden and cried. How could she be happy in the desert?

The next morning, Kester woke Anya and led her to the window.

"Look, Anya!" said Kester. "The old man did keep his promise."

Anya looked out the window. As far as the eye could see was her garden. The familiar green plants and flowers and fountains covered the dry sand.

"It isn't important where you live, Anya," said the prince. "You will always have your garden."

Story Summary and Language

Irregular verbs: Here are the present and irregular past-tense forms of some verbs:

Present	Past	Present	Past
choose	chose	leave	left
fall	fell	ride	rode
give	gave	see	saw
grow	grew	tell	told
is	was	wake	woke
keep	kept	go	went

Complete the story summary. Use the irregular verbs from the box.

chose	fell	rode	kept	was	gave
saw	woke	told	went	grew	left

Anya lived in a beautiful garden in India. She _____ very happy
there. A guru _____ her one wish. Anya _____ to live all her life in
                    B   C
her garden. The young girl _____ up and became a beautiful woman.
                            D
Many men _____ in love with her. Anya _____ them all to go away.
          E   F
She wanted to stay in her garden.

    One day she _____ a stranger. She fell in love with Prince Kester.
                        G
She _____ her garden and _____ with the prince. They _____ camels
     H   I   J
to Kester's home in the desert. His palace was elegant, but there was
no green anywhere. Anya cried that night, thinking about her garden.

    In the morning, Kester _____ his wife. "Look! The old man
                              K
_____ his promise." Anya's garden was there, all around the palace.
  L

Deeper Understanding

Answer the questions.

1. How did the garden make Anya feel?
2. Describe your favorite place in nature. How does that place make you feel?
3. The guru said to Anya, "Maybe someday you will want more than a garden." Was he correct? Explain.
4. How can we keep the things we love with us?
5. Write down your favorite sentences from the story. Why did you choose them?
6. How did you solve the problem of moving to a new place? How was the problem in the story solved? Compare the two solutions.

Theme

Complete this sentence about the story's main idea.

Happiness is _____.

BEYOND

Game

Play Hangman with vocabulary from the story. Each person writes five difficult words on a piece of paper. One person collects the words and chooses one. He or she writes spaces on the board for the letters of the word. The other people guess the missing letters of the word.

Project

Find a picture of nature in a magazine. Write some sentences about the picture. Use clear details. Here is an example:

There are hundreds of gold fish. All of them are swimming in the same direction. It is deep in the ocean. The water is a bright blue.

Then make the sentences into a poem. When you have finished, put the picture and the poem on a piece of colored paper. Here is an example of a finished poem:

Harmony

Deep down in the ocean
In the bright blue water
Hundreds of gleaming, golden fish
All swim in the same direction.

Role-Play

These lines are from a scene in the story. The guru comes to Anya's garden. He wants to give her a wish. Role-play with a partner. Finish the scene with two or more lines.

Guru: I knew your mother. I promised her that I would give you one wish.

Anya: What wish can I choose?

Guru:

Anya:

 Talk

Knowing the Area

"Talk" is a folktale from the Ashanti people in Africa.

GHANA

1. Name two continents near the continent of Africa.
2. Today, the Ashanti people live in the country Ghana. Ghana is in the northwestern part of Africa. Which ocean is near this country?

Vocabulary

These are people and items in the land of the Ashantis. Match the item with the person.

People	Items
___ 1. farmer	A. river
___ 2. weaver	B. stool
___ 3. fisherman	C. cloth
___ 4. swimmer	D. yam (like a potato)
___ 5. chief	E. fishing net

Problem Solving

In the folktale "Talk," a yam begins to talk. Pretend that you find a talking yam. You tell people about the yam. But no one believes you. List three or more ways to solve this problem.

Journal

Why do only people talk? Why don't animals, plants, or objects talk?

THROUGH

This folktale tells about a farmer and his talking yam.

A farmer went to his field one morning to dig up some yams. He wanted to eat the yams for dinner. As he was digging, a yam spoke to him. "Hey, what are you doing with your stick? Go away and leave me alone."

The farmer turned around and looked at his cow. The cow was eating grass. The man was amazed. "Did you say something?"

The cow kept eating. But the man's dog spoke. "It wasn't the cow. It was the yam. The yam wants you to go away."

The man was angry. The dog had never spoken before. The farmer also didn't like the dog's tone of voice. He decided to hit his dog with a branch. Using his knife, the man cut a branch off a palm tree. At that moment, the palm tree spoke. "Don't cut my branch!"

The man was very upset. He didn't like what was happening. He threw the branch on the ground. The palm branch said, "Hey, put me down softly!"

The farmer carefully put the branch down on a stone. But the stone yelled, "Man, take that branch off me!"

By now, the farmer was scared to death. He started to run to the village. On the path, he met a fisherman. The fisherman was carrying a fishing net.

"What's the problem?" asked the fisherman.

The farmer told his story about the talking yam, dog, tree, branch, and stone. "What a crazy story! That's no reason to be scared," said the fisherman.

The man's fishing net asked the farmer, "Well, did you take the branch off the stone?"

"Yikes!" yelled the fisherman. He threw the fishing net on the ground. Both he and the farmer ran down the path. They met a weaver. The weaver was carrying cloth on her head. "Where are you going so fast? You almost hit me," she said.

The farmer told the woman his story about the talking yam, dog, tree, branch, and stone. The fisherman told her about the talking fishing net. "You foolish men! I don't believe you. What a crazy reason to run," said the weaver.

"I think you'd run," said the cloth on her head.

"Oh, no!" shouted the weaver. She dropped her cloth. Then she ran after the farmer and the fisherman.

The three came to a river. They began to cross the water. In the river, a man was swimming. "What are you doing? Are you hunting an animal?" the man asked.

The farmer told his story about the talking yam, dog, tree, branch, and stone. The fisherman told about the talking fishing net. The weaver told about her talking cloth. "That's a crazy story! Forget it and take a swim," said the swimmer.

"You'd run if that happened," said the river. The man jumped out of the river. He began to run with the other people.

At last they came to the village. All four ran to the house of the chief. The chief's servant brought out the chief's stool. The chief sat on his stool and listened to the people.

The farmer told his story about the talking yam, dog, tree, branch, and stone. The fisherman told about the talking fishing net. The weaver told about her talking cloth. The swimmer told about the talking river.

The chief was patient at first. Then he became angry.

"I don't believe one word. Go back to work before I punish you. You are wasting my time."

The three men and the woman sadly walked away. The chief was still angry. "Foolish talk can upset the whole village," said the chief.

"What a story!" said the stool. "That's crazy, a talking yam!"

Deeper Understanding

Answer the questions.

1. Why was the farmer angry at his dog?
2. Why were the farmer, the fisherman, the weaver, and the swimmer scared by the talking objects?
3. What do you think the chief did after the stool talked?
4. Do you wish objects could talk? Explain.
5. Find a funny line in the story. Read it to a partner or write it down.
6. How did you solve the problem of the talking yam? How did the farmer try to solve the problem? Compare the two solutions.

Theme

Complete this sentence about the story's main idea.

To believe something, most people _____.

Story Language

Rewrite these sentences about the story. Mark them this way:

- Put a comma before the quotation.
- Put quotation marks before and after what is said.
- Put a capital letter at the beginning of the quotation.
- Put the period before the last quotation mark.

Here are examples of an unmarked sentence and a marked sentence:

The yam said go away and leave me alone.
The yam said, "Go away and leave me alone."

1. The dog said it wasn't the cow.
2. The palm tree told him don't cut my branch.
3. The palm branch said put me down softly.
4. The stone yelled take that branch off me.
5. The fisherman said what a crazy story.

6. The cloth said I think you'd run.
7. The chief said I don't believe one word.
8. The stool said that's crazy, a talking yam.

BEYOND

Game

Play Twenty Questions. Every student writes down five words from the story. Then one student stands in front of the class. The others ask yes/no questions about each of the student's words until they guess the word. Take turns in front of the class.

Project

Choose a place with many objects: your house, your bedroom, the classroom, or inside a car. Then pretend that the objects in the place are speaking to each other. Write the conversation. Here is an example:

My Kitchen

Refrigerator: Close my door! I'm cold.

Oven: You're always cold.

Refrigerator: And you're too hot.

Role-Play

This is a scene from the end of the story. The chief doesn't believe in talking objects. Role-play with a partner. Tell what happens next.

Chief: Foolish talk can upset the whole village.

Stool: What a story! That's crazy, a talking yam!

Chief:

Stool:

Little Havroshechka _____

Knowing the Area

"Little Havroshechka" is a Russian folktale. Russia is one of the states in the Commonwealth of Independent States (the former Soviet Union).

RUSSIAN FEDERATION

1. Russia is on two continents. What are the two continents?
2. Name two countries next to Russia.

Cluster

In the story "Little Havroshechka," the young girl is an orphan. An orphan has no parents. What does *orphan* make you think of? Write the words by the lines.

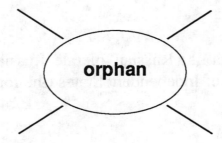

orphan

Problem Solving

In the story "Little Havroshechka," the girl has to do a huge amount of work in one day. Imagine that this is your problem.

What will you do? List three or more ways to solve this problem.

THROUGH

This Russian folktale is about an unhappy orphan.

Little Havroshechka

Little Havroshechka was an orphan. She had no parents. A family took Havroshechka to their home. They wanted her to be their servant. The girl worked all the time.

In the house, there were three daughters. The girls were called One-Eye, Two-Eyes, and Three-Eyes. The three sisters did nothing all day. They just sat and watched people walk by. They never said a kind word to Havroshechka.

One day, Havroshechka went outside to see her cow. "Oh, you are my only friend," she said. "The mistress and her daughters hit me and yell at me. They don't give me enough food. I have to work all day without rest. The mistress says I must have five pieces of cloth by tomorrow. If not, I get no dinner."

The cow loved Havroshechka. She said, "I will help you." Suddenly, five pieces of cloth appeared. The cow was a magic cow. Havroshechka took the cloth to her mistress. The mistress said, "You are finished? Then I will give you more work. I want ten pieces of cloth by tomorrow."

Little Havroshechka told the cow her problem. This time, the cow made ten pieces of cloth. Again the girl took the cloth to her mistress.

The mistress said nothing to Havroshechka. The girl left the room. "Daughters, come here," said the mistress. "Someone is helping Havroshechka. One-Eye, go and see who helps the girl."

One-Eye went with Havroshechka to the fields. The daughter lay down on the grass. Little Havroshechka sang, "Sleep, little eye, sleep!" One-Eye shut her eye and fell asleep. As she slept, the cow made the cloth.

Next, the mistress sent Two-Eyes to watch Little Havroshechka. Two-Eyes also lay down on the grass. Havroshechka sang, "Sleep, little eye! Sleep, other little eye!" Two-Eyes fell asleep.

This time, the mistress sent Three-Eyes to watch Havroshechka. This daughter also lay down on the grass. Havroshechka sang, "Sleep, little eye! Sleep, the other little eye!" She forgot all about the third eye. Two of Three-Eyes' eyes fell alseep. But the third one saw everything.

The daughter went home. She told her mother about the magic cow. The woman told her husband, "Go and kill the cow."

Havroshechka heard her mistress talking. The girl went to the cow. "They want to kill you!" she said. The girl was crying.

The cow answered, "Don't be sad. After I die, take my bones. Bury them in a garden. And water them every day."

Little Havroshechka followed the cow's directions. After the cow was killed, she took the bones. She buried them in the garden. And she watered them every day.

A beautiful apple tree began to grow in the garden. In a few years, it had delicious apples. And the tree had leaves of gold. Everyone came to see the special tree.

A long time later, a young man came by. He saw the three daughters watching the road. "Girls! I will marry the one who brings me an apple off that special tree."

The young man was rich and handsome. The three girls hurried to the tree. Each tried to pick an apple. But the tree would not let the girls pick the apples. The tree swung the apples high in the air. The girls tried and tried. Still, they couldn't get the apples.

Then Havroshechka walked to the tree. Instantly, an apple fell into her hands. She gave the apple to the young man. Havroshechka and the young man married soon after. From that day on, the girl knew no more sadness.

Story Summary and Language

Write the words in the correct order. Make sentences. The sentences are a summary of the story.

1. with a / Havroshechka / lived / cruel family / .
2. without rest / all day / had to work / Havroshechka / .
3. helped Havroshechka / a cow / to make cloth / .
4. her daughters / the mistress / to watch Havroshechka / sent / .
5. slept / except for / all the daughters / Three-Eyes / .
6. killed / the magic cow / the mistress's husband / .
7. Havroshechka / in a garden / buried / the cow's bones / .
8. grew / a beautiful magic apple tree / from the bones / .
9. from the tree / Havroshechka / gave an apple / to a young man / .
10. and lived happily / Havroshechka / married / the rich young man / .

Deeper Understanding

Answer the questions.

1. Why did the family want Havroshechka to live with them?
2. How did the mistress know that someone helped Havroshechka?
3. Where did the magic tree come from?
4. What unusual or impossible things happened in this story? List three or more.
5. Find one or more sentences from the story that tell about something unusual. Read them to a partner or write them in your journal. Why did you choose these sentences?
6. How did you solve the problem of too much work? How did Havroshechka solve her problem? Compare the two solutions. Which solution do you like better?

Theme

Havroshechka's best friend was a cow. The cow helped her. Complete this sentence about the story's main idea.

A friend _____.

BEYOND

Game

Work in pairs. Each person picks eight words from the story. Find words that can be described in a picture. The first person chooses one word. He or she does not tell the word. The first person tells the partner how to draw a picture of the word. The partner draws and guesses the word. Take turns giving directions and drawing pictures.

Project

Divide the class into small groups. Each group draws a large picture of one scene from the story. (You may use the scenes described in Story Summary and Language.) Put the big pictures on the bulletin board in the correct order.

Role-Play

In the beginning of the story, Havroshechka tells the cow about her problems. Role-play with a partner. Finish the scene.

Havroshechka: You are my only friend. The mistress and her daughters hit me and yell at me.

Cow: Maybe I can help you.

Havroshechka: I must make five pieces of cloth before tomorrow.

Cow:

Havroshechka:

The Lesson

Knowing the Area

"The Lesson" is a folktale from Mexico.

MEXICO

1. On which continent is Mexico?
2. Name two countries next to Mexico.

Cluster

The folktale "The Lesson" tells about a very jealous man. Draw a cluster for *jealousy*. What people and actions go with the idea of jealousy? Write the words.

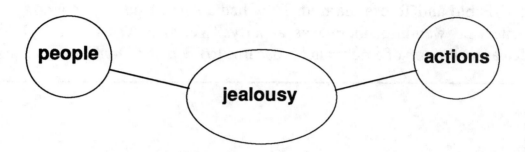

Problem Solving

In the story "The Lesson," a man is very jealous of his wife. Pretend that your girlfriend or boyfriend is too jealous. List three or more ways to solve this problem.

Journal

Why are some people too jealous? List three or more reasons.

THROUGH

In this Mexican folktale, a man is very jealous of his wife.

The Lesson

In Mexico, there once lived a man named Pablo. The man was very jealous of his pretty girlfriend. He had no reason to be jealous. Teresa was not interested in other men. She loved only Pablo.

Pablo and Teresa married. They had a small wedding in a church. After the wedding, there was a party. Everyone was dancing. Don Ricardo, the son of a rich ranchero, came to the party. Don Ricardo liked

pretty ladies. He asked the bride for a dance. It is a custom for people to dance with the bride.

Later, everyone went home. Teresa said, "What a wonderful day!"

But Pablo was angry. "Did you like dancing with that rich man? Did you make a date with him?" Teresa started to cry. She couldn't understand Pablo. She had done nothing wrong.

A month later, the couple went for a walk. They passed Don Ricardo on the road. "Good afternoon, Señora," said the rich man. Teresa turned her head away. She said nothing to Don Ricardo. But her husband was still angry.

"Get all your things. We are moving tomorrow. I don't want to live in the same town with Don Ricardo."

They left the next day. Pablo and Teresa moved to a small town in the north. They rented a little house. Pablo found a job. They saved money to buy a cow. On a farm close by there was a bull. The cow and bull met and fell in love. They were together all the time.

A candy man started to pass by Pablo's house. The young man was very handsome. Teresa bought candy from him every day. One day, Pablo came home early. He saw Teresa talking to the candy seller.

At home, Pablo yelled, "What happens when I go to work? Are you seeing this man every day?"

By now, the wife was tired of her husband's jealousy. "You are making us miserable! I am always true to you. You have no reason to be jealous. I am losing my patience. Stop being so jealous!" The husband and wife had a big fight. Pablo decided to move again.

Two days later, they were on the road. Teresa didn't want to move. She was unhappy. The cow came with the couple.

After a few miles, the cow began to moo. "What's wrong with that cow?" asked Pablo. His wife told Pablo about the bull. The cow did not want to leave her loved one. The wife calmed the cow.

After a few more miles, the cow began to moo again. The wife calmed her for a while. But in a few moments, the cow was mooing loudly.

In the evening, the couple made a camp. The cow was mooing louder than ever. "That noisy cow is giving me a headache! Tell her to be quiet, or I will leave her here."

Teresa went to the cow. "Quiet! There will be other bulls in the new town!"

Pablo heard his wife talking. He thought about his wife's words. "There will be other bulls in the new town." He couldn't stop thinking. He didn't sleep all night.

After that night, Pablo changed. He said, "We're going back home again." Teresa was delighted with Pablo's change. They returned to their old house. And the cow and the bull lived happily ever after.

Story Summary and Language

Adjectives: *Adjectives* are words that describe nouns. Here are some examples of adjectives:

a *pretty* lady   a *new* house   a *noisy* cow

Complete the story summary. Use the adjectives from the box.

new	other	handsome	rich
jealous	happy	miserable	old

Pablo and Teresa married. At the wedding party, Teresa danced with a _____ man. Pablo was _____. He decided to move away from

     A   B
the man. The next day, they went to a _____ town. Pablo bought a

           C
cow. The cow fell in love with a bull.

One day, Pablo saw Teresa talking to a _____ candy man. He

       D
yelled at Teresa. She said, "You are making us _____!"

       E

Pablo decided to move again. On the road the cow mooed loudly. Teresa told the cow, "There will be _____ bulls in the new town."

       F
Pablo thought about his wife's words. He decided to move back to their _____ home. Teresa was _____. So were the cow and the bull.

     G   H

Deeper Understanding

Answer the questions.

1. What problem did Pablo have?
2. What did Pablo do every time a man looked at his wife?
3. Pablo needed to change. How did he realize that?
4. Who suffers more, the jealous person or the loved one of the jealous person? Explain.

5. Find one or more important lines in the story. Read them to a partner or write them down. Why did you choose these lines?

6. How did you solve the problem of jealousy? How was the problem in the story solved? Compare the two solutions.

Theme

Complete this sentence about the story's main idea.

Jealousy is _____.

BEYOND

Game

Find six words from the story. Put the letters of each word in the wrong order. Then find a partner. Put the letters of your partner's words in the correct order.

Project

Find words and pictures about ideas in the story. Look for them in magazines and newspapers. Then make a collage with the words and pictures.

Role-Play

This is a scene from the middle of the story. Pablo and Teresa are talking about the candy man. Role-play with a partner. Finish the scene.

Pablo: Are you and the candy man seeing each other every day?

Teresa: I only buy candy from him!

Pablo:

Teresa:

Charan

Knowing the Area

"Charan" is a tale from Korea. It may be a true love story from AD 1400.

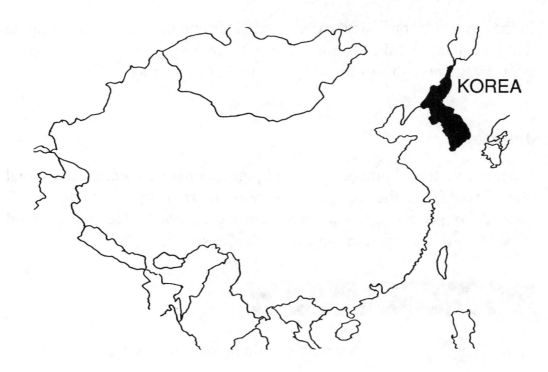

KOREA

1. Is Korea on the continent of Africa, Asia, Australia, Europe, North America, or South America?
2. Today, Korea is two countries. Name the two countries.
3. What country is north of North Korea?
4. What land is east of North Korea and South Korea?

Cause and Effect

The young man in the story travels a long way in the snow. He has many problems. Match the problems with their possible results.

Problems	Possible Results
___ 1. long trip	A. hungry
___ 2. no food	B. must beg for money
___ 3. no money	C. may freeze to death
___ 4. cold; no warm clothes	D. very tired

Problem Solving

In the story "Charan," a boyfriend and girlfriend must separate. Imagine that your parents said you must move away from your loved one. How would you solve this problem? List three or more ways.

Journal

In some countries, both today and long ago, people are separated by social class. People from the lower class are not to marry people from the higher class. Also, people of lower class cannot get a good education or good jobs. Does this happen in the U.S. today? Explain.

THROUGH

In this Korean story, two young people in love must separate.

Charan

The governor of Pyong-an Province in Korea had only one child. His son's name was Keydong. The young man was an excellent student and writer. On Keydong's sixteenth birthday, the governor gave his son a big party. At the party, there were many dancing girls. One lovely girl named Charan danced with Keydong. Everyone enjoyed watching the handsome couple dance.

That night, the young man and woman fell in love. They began to see each other every day. They talked together many hours. They became best friends.

Six years later, the king wanted the governor to become his chief justice. The governor and his family had to move to Seoul.

The governor spoke to his son. "Keydong, we must move. I see that you love Charan. But you cannot marry the girl. You know that. She is not from your social class."

"Father, don't worry," said Keydong. "I understand. I will tell Charan good-bye."

The young girl cried on the day of parting. But Keydong showed no emotion on his face.

Keydong went to Seoul with his family. He tried to forget Charan. But he could not. When he studied, he thought only of his love. One night in the middle of winter, he left his home. He wanted to return to Charan.

In the morning, Keydong's mother went to talk to her son. The young man was gone. His mother and father didn't know where he was. Everyone looked for the young man. At last the parents decided Keydong was dead. Maybe a tiger had eaten him. The parents sadly burned their son's clothes in a death ceremony.

Keydong's trip to Pyong-an was very hard. Charan lived hundreds of miles away. There was snow on the road. Keydong was a rich man's son. He had never known hunger or cold before. He had to beg for food. He nearly froze to death. He walked in the snow for one month.

Finally, Keydong arrived in Pyong-an. He found Charan. She cried in joy to see her love again. The two decided to run away together.

Keydong and Charan married. Then they went to live in a mountain village. Keydong became a servant. Charan sewed clothes to sell. They were very poor, but the two were happy.

Then one day, Charan spoke to her husband. "You left your parents. They don't know that you are alive. This is wrong. But you cannot return home. What can we do?"

"I don't know," said Keydong sadly.

"I have an idea. You can study for the official exam. If you pass, you bring honor to yourself. You can see your parents again. You will also become a state official."

Keydong agreed to the plan. They bought books for him to study. Every night, the two sat by the light of a candle. Charan sewed and Keydong studied. Two years passed in this way.

At last Keydong and Charan went to Seoul for the big exam. Keydong wrote beautifully on his test. He won first place.

The king asked to see Keydong. "You are the winner of the exam. That is excellent. But I don't understand one thing. You wrote that you are the son of my chief justice. His only son died three years ago."

Keydong told his story. The king said, "I forgive you for your wrong actions. I will not punish you for your love. Charan is no common person. I will make her equal in social class to you."

Keydong went to see his parents. The parents were filled with happiness to see their son again. Keydong and Charan officially married in a big festival. Later, Keydong became one of Korea's first men of state. He and Charan lived a long, happy life.

Story Summary and Language

Rewrite the paragraphs below. Add the missing periods. Begin each new sentence with a capital letter. Remember, each sentence needs a subject and a verb.

A governor in Korea had a son named Keydong the son fell in love with a dancing girl one day Keydong had to move to Seoul with his family Keydong couldn't forget his girlfriend he walked hundreds of miles to see her he nearly died in the cold snow Keydong's parents believed their son was dead

Charan was very happy to see Keydong the two married they ran away to live in a mountain village Charan and Keydong were sad about Keydong's parents Charan had an idea she told Keydong to study for the official exam Keydong studied for two years at last he took the test he won first place the king forgave Keydong the young man saw his parents again Keydong and Charan lived a long, happy life

Deeper Understanding

Answer the questions.

1. According to the father, why shouldn't Keydong marry Charan?
2. How do you know that Keydong loved Charan very much? Explain.
3. How did Charan help Keydong?
4. Describe two qualities of Keydong's personality and two qualities of Charan's personality.
5. Do you think Keydong's parents forgave Keydong for his wrong actions? Explain.
6. Find one or more lines from the story that tell about Keydong's personality. Who does he remind you of? Read the lines to a partner or write them down.
7. How did you solve the problem of moving away from your loved one? How did Keydong try to solve the problem? Compare the two solutions.

Theme

Complete this sentence about the main idea of the story.

If two people love each other, social class _____.

BEYOND

Game

Divide the class into two teams. Each team chooses three or more important sentences from the story. An example is, "They became best friends." Mark spaces on the chalkboard for the words in each sentence. Then play Hangman with the sentences.

Project

Write a newspaper article about Keydong, the winner of the official exam. Tell who, what, when, where, and why in the article.

Role-Play

This is a scene from the end of the story. Keydong sees his father again after three years. Role-play with a partner. Finish the scene with two or more lines.

Keydong: Father, I am happy to see you again.

Father: Where were you?

Keydong:

Father:

Canyon of Sorrows_____

Knowing the Area

"Canyon of Sorrows" is a folktale from Japan.

JAPAN

1. Is Japan closest to the continent of Africa, Asia, Australia, Europe, North America, or South America?
2. Which ocean is east of Japan?
3. Name two countries near Japan.

Cluster

What do the words *older people* make you think of? Write your ideas by the lines.

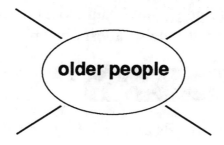

Chart

Complete the chart below. Work alone, with a partner, or in a group.

Things or services that older people can give us	Things or services that we can give older people

Problem Solving

In the folktale "Canyon of Sorrows," the lord of the land has a law: All people sixty (60) years of age must die.

Imagine that your grandfather is sixty years old. You must take him to a canyon and leave him. There he will die. You don't want to do this. List three or more ways to solve this problem.

Vocabulary

Look at the pictures in the story. Point to an **ant**, a **thread**, a **conch shell**, a tree **branch**, **ashes**, and a **rope**. Then write the words for these objects in order of size. Start with the smallest object.

THROUGH

This folktale from Japan tells of a time long ago. Then, old people were not respected.

Canyon of Sorrows

Long, long ago in Japan, old age was not respected. When men and women turned sixty years old, they were taken up a mountain. Then they were thrown down into the canyon below. The old people were left to die in the Canyon of Sorrows.

During those years, there lived an old farmer. One spring, he turned sixty years old. By the law, it was time for the old man to die. The lord of the country always carried out this law.

The farmer's son said sadly, "Father, it is time. I must take you to the canyon. The lord's men will visit our village soon. If they find you, they will kill you. And they will kill me, too, because I broke the law." The son had tears in his eyes. He loved the old man very much. The son's wife began to cry loudly. She gave the old man a kiss.

The son carried his old father on his back. The old man couldn't climb the mountain by himself. He wasn't strong enough. On the way up the mountain, the old man broke off the ends of tree branches. He did this to mark the way.

"Father, why are you doing that? Why are you marking the way? Do you plan to return home? You know you cannot," said the son.

"No, my son," said the old farmer. "I am marking the way for you. I don't want you to lose your way home."

The son stopped walking. He began to cry at his father's kindness. "Father, we must return home. I cannot do this to you. I will hide you."

The son carried the old man home. He hid his father under the house. The lord's men wouldn't find him there.

The lord of the country liked to make life difficult for his people. One day, he called the farmers together. He said, "You must each bring me a rope. Make the rope from ashes."

All the farmers were worried. They could not make a rope from ashes. The ashes would fall apart. What would the lord do if no one followed his order?

The son told his father of the lord's command. The father answered from under the house. "Son, you must first make a fine, strong rope. Burn it until it turns to ashes. Then carefully take the rope of ashes to the lord."

The son followed the directions. He took the rope of ashes to the lord. None of the other farmers had done it. "Excellent!" said the lord to the young farmer. "Now I have another job for all of you. Bring me a conch shell. The shell must have a thread passed through it."

The young farmer went to his father again. "Son, first find a conch shell," said the father. "Place the opening toward the light. Next, put rice on the end of a thread. Give the rice to an ant. Place the ant in the shell. The ant will go through and take the thread with him."

The son did as he was told. Again, the father was right. The farmer took the shell to the lord. The lord was amazed and happy. "How did you do this? You are very wise. I want to honor you."

The young man looked down at the ground. "This honor is not for me, my lord. My old father is the wise one. He told me what to do. My father is sixty years old. It was time to throw him down the canyon. I couldn't do it. He is now hiding under my house."

The lord was quiet. Then he said, "Bring your father to me."

The son was afraid. Was the lord going to kill his father? He sadly brought his father to the lord.

"You are a wise man," said the lord to the old farmer. "You know a great deal. You are not strong, but you are wise. Maybe it is a bad idea to throw old people in the canyon. You are old. Still, you have much to offer." On that day, the lord changed the law. Old people were not left in the canyon anymore.

Story Summary and Language

Possessive nouns: A *possessive noun* has this form:

(noun) + 's

Here are two examples of possessive nouns:

the son of the farmer = the farmer's son
the men of the lord = the lord's men

Complete the story summary. Use the possessive nouns from the box.

son's wife	lord's law	farmer's son	lord's men
father's ideas	son's house	son's way	father's kindness

Long, long ago in Japan, old age wasn't respected. By the _____,
<u>A</u>
at age sixty, people were thrown in a canyon. An old farmer turned
sixty years old. The _____ said, "I must take you to the canyon. If not,
<u>B</u>
the _____ will kill you and me." The _____ cried loudly.
<u>C</u>   <u>D</u>
On the way to the canyon, the old farmer marked his _____ with
<u>E</u>
three branches. The son cried at his _____. The young farmer
<u>F</u>
returned home with his father. The old man was hidden under the
_____.
<u>G</u>
As a game, the lord asked all the farmers some difficult questions.
Using his _____, the son solved the problems. The young farmer
<u>H</u>
honestly told the lord, "My old father answered the questions." The
lord then decided to change the law. He realized that old people still
have much to offer.

Deeper Understanding

Answer the questions.

1. Why do you think the lord didn't want old people in his land?
2. Why didn't the son obey the law of the lord?
3. Is the son an honest man? Give proof for your answer.
4. The lord finally realized that old people have special quality. What is this quality?
5. How did the lord treat old people at first? How do the Japanese treat old people today? Compare the two approaches.
6. How did you solve the problem of leaving your grandfather? How did the son solve the problem of leaving his father? Compare the two solutions.

Theme

Complete this sentence about the main idea of the story.

It's important to respect old people because _____.

BEYOND

Interview

Interview an older member of your family. What things has he or she learned in life? Share this information with a partner or the class.

Game

On a piece of paper, draw a large tic-tac-toe game with nine squares. Write these words in the squares: *shell, thread, ant, rope, ashes, branch, canyon, rice,* and *farmer.* Play with a partner, in small groups, or as a class. To mark an X or O, point correctly to the picture of the word in the story.

Project

Draw a picture of an older person you respect. Then write about the person. Use this form:

This is _____. I respect _____ because _____.

Role-Play

Here are two lines from a scene from the story. The lord wants to honor the young farmer for his good ideas. Role-play with a partner. Finish the scene with two or more lines.

Lord: You are very wise. I want to honor you.

Son: The honor is not for me. My father is the wise one.

Lord:

Son: